S0-BSP-703

1998

—— D.J. Lightfoot ——

TRAIL FEVER
The Life of a Texas Cowboy
—— Illustrated by John Bobbish ——

Lothrop, Lee & Shepard Books   **New York**

To WILLIAM E. "BILL" JARY, JR. (1911–1989),
who told me so much about his grandpa,
George Saunders,
I had to write a book;
and to ROLAND SAUNDERS JARY,
whose long roundup of facts
about his great-grandpa
got me headed up the trail
in the right direction.

First Edition   1 2 3 4 5 6 7 8 9 10

Library of Congress Cataloging in Publication
Lightfoot, D. J. Trail fever : the life of a Texas cowboy / by D.J. Lightfoot ; illustrated by John Bobbish
p.   cm. Includes bibliographical references. Summary: A biography of George Saunders, a cowboy who endured cattle drives, stampedes, and skirmished with Indians on the Texas frontier during and after the Civil War. ISBN 0-688-11537-3 1. Saunders, George W. (George Washington), 1854–1933—Juvenile fiction. [1. Saunders, George W. (George Washington), 1854–1933—Fiction. 2. Cowboys—Fiction. 3. Texas—Fiction. 4. Frontier and pioneer life—Texas—Fiction. 5. West (U.S.)—Fiction.] I. Bobbish, John, ill. II. Title. PZ7.L6257Tr 1992 [Fic]—dc20 92-5458 CIP AC

Contents

Always a Cowboy	1
Life on Lost Creek	8
Stampede!	16
School Days	22
Trail Fever	29
Up the "Chizzum" Trail	37
Bandits!	47
The Last Trail	57
The Trail Drivers of Texas	68
Bibliography	73

Always a Cowboy

Georke Washington Saunders had always been a cowboy—as far as he knew. There may have been a time when he was too young, but he couldn't remember that. He could ride a horse before he could walk. And by the time he was five, he could herd cattle from horseback almost as well as his three big brothers, Mat, Bill, and Jack. He proved it the year his family moved.

The Saunderses lived near the small South

1

Texas town of Rancho. That's where George was born, on February 12, 1854. But George's father wanted a better place to live, with better land for raising cattle. Farther south, in Goliad County, he found what he wanted on a little stream called Lost Creek. The stream ran through brushy grassland that was perfect for a cattle ranch.

"Get your horses, boys," Mr. Saunders told George and Jack one morning in 1859. "Go find your brothers. We're moving down on Lost Creek."

George and Jack ran to catch their ponies. Jack caught his first. He saddled up and rode away to find Mat and Bill, who were off tending the family's cattle. George needed a saddle, too, but the only one left was his sister Nancy's sidesaddle.

Nancy agreed to let George use it. "If you think you won't fall off," she teased.

"I won't neither fall off!" cried George. "You wait and see."

When his brothers returned, George was ready to ride. But when they saw George perched atop Nancy's sidesaddle, they laughed so hard that they nearly fell off their horses.

"Never mind them," Mr. Saunders told George. "Show 'em how you can ride."

The sidesaddle was hard to straddle, but George hung on. He went with his brothers to gather the Saunders herd.

While they were gone, Nancy and sister Sarah Ann helped their mother and father load the wagon. Their furniture was made of pine and cedar wood, so it wasn't too heavy to move. In the bottom of the open wagon box, they put the bedsteads, chest of drawers, kitchen hutch, table, and eight chairs. On top of these went the spinning wheel. They wrapped it carefully to protect it from bumps and jolts. Next came bedding, bundles of clothes, and kitchen utensils. On top of everything went cooking pots, blankets, and supplies the family would need during the trip. To keep out rain and dust, they stretched a waterproof tarpaulin over the load.

When all was ready, the family started south. The girls rode in the wagon with Mrs. Saunders and the little ones, Steven Allen and baby John Calhoun. Mr. Saunders and the boys rode ahead with the cattle to guide them and keep them from straying. The herd of three hundred longhorns strung out for nearly a quarter of a mile across the prairie. It didn't matter that George was only five or that he rode his sister's sidesaddle. He had the important job of trailing behind and keeping up the tail end of the herd.

At first the trip went well. The cattle ambled slowly over the meadows and through open clusters of live oak and mesquite trees. They paused often to graze the tall bunchgrass and drink from the small streams that crossed their path. The caravan traveled only about ten miles a day. Mr. Saunders didn't want to hurry the cows with young calves, or the steers he was fattening to butcher. Even at their slow pace, the fifty-mile trip to Lost Creek should not take more than four or five days.

But then, only a few miles from their new home, the travelers came to the fast-flowing waters of the San Antonio River. To get across, the cattle would have to swim.

Mr. Saunders had a plan. "I'll swim my horse across first," he said. "Then you boys drive the beeves into the river. They will follow me."

George and his brothers rode in tight at the sides and back of the herd. They pressed closer until the cattle had nowhere to go except into the water. The animals swam strongly for the far bank. They tried to follow Mr. Saunders. But the fast current caught many and swept them downstream.

Mrs. Saunders cried out, "The cattle are drowning! We're going to lose them!"

Mat and Bill plunged their horses into the river and headed for the other side. George looked at Jack. Before their mother could stop them, the boys followed. George got a mouthful of water as his horse nearly went under in the swift current. The pony kicked hard, fighting to stay above water. George hung on with all his strength as his pony swam to the far bank.

As soon as George and Jack clambered onto the riverbank, they turned downstream and kicked their horses into a run. Mr. Saunders, Mat, and Bill had already caught up with some of the cattle. The beeves had struggled to the bank and pulled themselves out of the water. They stood dripping wet. Their sides heaved as they caught their breath.

George and Jack guarded that bunch while the other riders raced downriver after the rest of the herd. The chase went on for half a mile. One by one, the tired cattle swam to the riverbank and climbed out. Each found a rider waiting. Not one longhorn drowned.

George, just five years old, did a grown cowboy's work that day. When all the herd was back on dry land, he helped drive the cattle to where Mrs. Saunders waited near the river. She had crossed at a ford where the water was shallow enough to drive the wagon over.

"We got 'em, Mother!" George yelled. "Every one of them."

"That's enough excitement for one day," Mr. Saunders said. "We'll camp here tonight. Tomorrow, we reach Lost Creek."

Life on Lost Creek

The homesite George's father had picked out on Lost Creek was a grassy plain dotted with mesquite trees, post oaks, and live oaks. There were many creeks and ponds. All of them brimmed with fish. Deer were everywhere. Opossums, skunks, and rabbits scurried through the brush. The land was wild and untouched.

Carving a home from the wilderness took many weeks of hard work. The family cut and hauled timber to build a log house and livestock pens. They camped out until their home was ready. Mat and Bill helped build the house. Nancy and Sarah Ann planted a vegetable garden and cooked meals over an open fire. George and Jack looked after the cattle.

One afternoon while the brothers rode herd, George spotted the biggest white-tailed deer he had ever seen. The buck stood at the edge of a clearing, half hidden by the branches of a live oak tree. It sniffed the breeze cautiously. So far it had not seen or scented the boys.

George stared in wonder. *"Jack,"* he hissed, *"look!"*

He should have kept quiet. The buck at once leaped for cover in the brush. Jack barely glimpsed the disappearing deer.

"It was a big ol' buck!" George exclaimed. "Big as a steer!"

Jack raised his eyebrows.

"Well," George said, "maybe not that big. But it was *awful* big."

Before Jack could argue, Mr. Saunders rode into the clearing, with a message: Mrs. Saunders wanted fish for supper. George and Jack

grinned at each other. In no time they were headed for the creek, fishing poles over their shoulders, hoping to catch a mess of bream.

Chirping birds and sparkling sun soon made George sleepy. He lay on the creek bank, eyes closed, waiting for a fish to bite. Nearby, a mockingbird sang. A mourning dove cooed. In the woods, a woodpecker hammered at a tree.

George sighed with happiness. "We must be living in Paradise," he told Jack.

But the days of Paradise did not last. In 1861, the Civil War started. The war was between the Union of the northern United States and the Confederacy of the southern states. Texas sided with the South.

Mr. Saunders and Mat left home the first

year of the war to fight in the Confederate Army. They mounted their horses, said a last good-bye, and disappeared into the trees. Mrs. Saunders began to cry. George ran to her.

"It'll be all right, Mother," he said quietly. "Jack and Bill and me, we'll take care of everything until Papa and Mat come home. You'll see."

But Bill soon left home, too. In 1862, he helped drive a herd of eight hundred longhorns to Mississippi. The cattle would feed the hungry soldiers of the Confederacy. Afterward, Bill also joined the Army of the South.

That left only eight-year-old George and eleven-year-old Jack to care for the cattle. It was the same all across Texas. Nearly every boy and man older than sixteen and younger than sixty went away to fight. The war bled Texas and the South dry of men and left the soldiers' wives and children to do the hard work of planting crops and tending cattle. Only a few men who were too old to fight stayed behind to help.

To make matters worse, supplies were nowhere to be found. The Saunderses and their neighbors could not buy the tools, medicines, bolts of cloth, leather shoes, or other things they needed. All those goods had to come into Texas from the outside world. But during the war, the North sent ships to choke off trade along the coast. The naval blockade meant that Texans could not sell their cotton or cattle, or buy dishes, cups, wax candles, knives, spoons, or any of the goods they once bought. Whatever they needed—hoes, nails, wagons, ox yokes, shoes, shirts, or hats—had to be made at home.

Everyone pitched in to help. Mrs. Saunders, Nancy, and Sarah Ann worked constantly to feed and clothe the family. They spun yarn on a spinning wheel and wove cloth on a loom. By taking turns, they kept the wheel and the loom moving from dawn to dark. They tilled a garden, tended the milk cows, churned butter, tanned leather, and looked after the little ones.

George and Jack spent nearly every waking hour in the saddle. They roped and branded their own calves and branded calves for neighbors who were away at war. They worked the prairies for miles around, and gave their neighbors a fair share of all the unbranded strays they found. On the open ranges, cattle drifted freely to water and good grazing. Stragglers got lost in the brush. It was an endless job for George and Jack to find their cattle and hold the herd loosely together. It also was the boys' job to drive away wild mustang horses. If their cow ponies mixed with them, the saddle horses soon became just as wild as the mustangs.

When he wasn't working cattle or chasing mustangs, George helped around the house. He learned to make the things that could no longer be bought. He whittled forks and spoons from wooden sticks. He made ropes from horsehair and hides that he tanned himself. He ground corn with a small hand gristmill and spun yarn until late at night. Often, he went to bed exhausted. The whole family did.

One morning, two years after Bill left for the army, George rode out with Jack to check on the cattle. In the pasture, he saw a yearling wearing the 1̂0 brand. He sat up straighter and his eyes shone. George owned that brand and the ten calves it marked.

He stopped for a good look while Jack rode on ahead. The "half circle ten" meant George was a cattleman in his own right. The "ten" in the brand was for his age and his ten calves. The curved line or "half circle" set his cattle apart from those of his brothers. They all had a few beeves of their own.

Whenever George saw one of his calves, it made him feel important and grown up. He could forget, for a moment, that his brothers and father were soldiers in a terrible war raging away to the east. *Someday I'll have a bunch more than ten calves!* he promised himself. Urging his pony into a trot, he hurried to catch up with Jack. His dreams could wait, but the day's work couldn't.

Stampede!

George rode to and fro in the night. He was edgy. He and about a dozen other cowboys were holding a herd of two hundred steers at a ranch near his home. At daybreak, the steers were to be driven to Mexico and traded for food and supplies. But this bunch of half-wild longhorns had the jitters. They milled around the pasture, restless and skittish. Such a spooky herd meant trouble.

Suddenly it happened. No one could say

what started it. A rabbit popping out of its hole, under the feet of a jumpy longhorn? An owl flying low overhead? A twig snapping with a loud *crack* under the hooves of a nervous steer?

Whatever the cause, it happened all at once. Instantly the still air of the Texas night was filled with a fury of sound. It rumbled. It thundered. George had never heard anything like the noise those cattle made. But he knew what it was. The frightened herd was running off in a panic. A stampede was on!

Two hundred steers bolted at a dead run, heading in six directions at once. They crashed through brush and dodged mesquite trees. George jabbed spurs to his horse. He raced after them, following the great noise they made.

Barely able to see in the gloom, George watched for low-hanging tree limbs and tangles of brush. They might knock him from his saddle. His sure-footed cow pony covered the rough, rolling ground at a gallop, staying close to the herd.

For hours, it seemed, the wild night ride went on. At first George could hear a few of the other cowboys nearby. "Whoop!" "Yah!" they yelled as they tried to turn the herd. Many of the riders were George's age—ten—or not much older. In 1864, the grown men were still far from home, fighting in the Civil War.

Twenty big Saunders steers were in the bunch that had just stampeded. The others belonged to the neighbors. His family and friends were counting on George to help deliver the herd. He had to stay with the runaways.

Racing through the darkness, George soon lost track of the other cowboys. He could hear nothing except the thud of his horse's hooves and the crash and rumble of the steers up ahead. He leaned forward and pressed close to his horse's neck so the tree limbs wouldn't hit him. But here and there, the branches slapped him hard and left deep scratches.

At last, tired from their run, the cattle began to slow. George reined his horse in and slowly rode up to the herd, careful not to spook them again.

In the faint moonlight, he could see only the steers and a few live oaks and mesquite trees. The tree limbs stood out like strange, spiky arms. Brush and prickly pear cactus threw

weird shadows on the grassland. There was no way to know how far or how long he had ridden, or even in which direction. For all George knew, he might be halfway to the San Antonio River or the Gulf of Mexico.

George closed his eyes and listened. He tried to hear a sound, any sound, from the other cowboys. Far off in the night, an owl hooted. Stirred by a slight breeze, the leathery leaves of the live oaks rustled softly. There was nothing else to hear except a few snuffles from the cattle.

I'm not scared, George told himself. *In the morning I can backtrack to the ranch.* He knew the stampeding cattle had left a trail of trampled brush and broken tree limbs. At daybreak, when it was light enough to see, he would drive his runaways back along that trail to the ranch.

George wiggled around, trying to get comfortable in his saddle. He had a long wait until dawn. He rubbed his arm where the rough bark of a live oak had scraped it. It was bleeding, just a little.

Things could have been far worse. If George's horse had stumbled, he could have been thrown hard to the ground. If he hadn't ducked, he might have been knocked from the saddle by a low limb. Sometimes men were trampled to death during stampedes. Others broke their necks. George had been lucky—this time.

School Days

On a warm spring evening in 1865, George's family sat down for their first meal together in four years. It was a night to celebrate. The Civil War was over, and George's father and brothers had come safely home.

Mr. Saunders, Mat, Bill, Nancy, Sarah Ann, Mrs. Saunders, George, Jack, and the youngest children pulled their chairs up to the table. It was weighted down with roast beef, corn-on-the-cob, string beans, and sweet potato pie.

Everybody dug in. They were all talking at once. George didn't try to speak over the babble. He knew he would have lots of time to visit with his dad and brothers in days to come.

Already that afternoon, they had gone for a short ride together to look at the cattle. Proudly, George showed them hundreds of longhorns wearing the Saunders brands. He and Jack had been careful to brand every new calf. They had looked after the herd so well during the war years that few strays had been lost. When Mat and Bill saw what a good job their little brothers had done, they thumped George and Jack on the back until the boys' shoulders ached. Mr. Saunders just smiled—and tried to hide his tears of happiness.

George was overjoyed to have his family together again. The return of his father and brothers took a big load off of him. He didn't have to work so hard on the ranch. But that gave him a new problem: Less ranch work meant more time for school work.

He didn't much like school. To his way of thinking, the only good thing about it was running horses during lunchtime. He lived only a mile from the country schoolhouse. He could have walked. But he needed his horse for the races. So, every morning before breakfast, he ran three or four miles, chasing down his pony so he could ride to school and be ready for the contests.

At the noon hour, George and his friends swung into their saddles. Someone yelped, "Yippee!" and the race was on. Grabbing his hat from his head, George swatted his pony's rump with it. Like a four-footed freight train, the horse sped for the finish line. George didn't always win, but he was always in the race.

Boys and girls on the Texas frontier generally didn't get much schooling. Most of them had to work on their family farms and ranches. George had chores to do, too, even after his father and brothers returned home. But with so many brothers and sisters to share the work, he had more time for school than a lot of Texans his age. Like it or not, he went whenever he could.

Part of the time when he was twelve and thirteen, he attended a boarding school about fifty miles away. Concrete College taught more

subjects than his neighborhood school. It had about a hundred students, girls as well as boys. The girls lived with the schoolmaster's family. The boys lived in two-room log cabins. Girls and boys did not eat together or have recess together.

George and the other pupils studied farming and ranching, music, penmanship, and grammar. They had math, geography, spelling, and foreign languages such as Hebrew, Greek, Latin, and German. The rules were strict. George had to get up at five in the morning. He had three hours to feed his horse, eat his own breakfast, and finish his lessons from the day before. The whole school attended church services at eight o'clock, then had classes until suppertime. George and his mates were supposed to spend most of the evening studying.

Everyone was required to dress neatly. Guns, bad language, drinking, dancing, gambling, and smoking were not allowed. Boys were whipped for fighting and could be expelled for wild parties.

The students went home between school terms. One time, George took some friends along to meet his family. As usual for going visiting, the boys wore their good clothes. George had on his only "Sunday-go-to-meeting" suit, with a starched paper collar at his neck.

The boys all sat on the front porch and talked. George sprawled on a narrow bench about two feet high. One of his friends dared him to roll off.

"Nothin' to it!" George declared. Not really meaning to roll, he made the motion to do it. But before he could catch himself, he hit the floor with a thud. The fall knocked the breath out of him. For a moment, he saw stars. He felt the other boys shaking him.

Suddenly, cold water hit him full in the face. Gasping for breath, he jumped up from the porch deck. There stood his brother Jack with an empty water bucket.

George looked down at his clothes. The only paper collar he owned was a squishy mess. The removable collar had been the dressiest part of his Sunday outfit. George exploded.

"You ruined my best suit! I'll fight every one of you! I'll take you all on, right now!"

The other boys were laughing too hard to fight, though. They rolled on the ground, holding their sides where they hurt from nonstop hee-haws.

Finally George grinned, too.

"Waal," he drawled, "I guess I do look pretty funny. But dang it all, that was my only paper collar!"

Trail Fever

George quit school when he was fourteen to become a full-time cowboy. The Civil War had ended three years before, and good times were returning to South Texas. He didn't want to miss a minute of the action. If the rumors were true, his family and the neighbor ranchers would not be strapped for cash much longer. Soon they might all be buying new Sunday suits.

Everyone was broke after the war. The soldiers had come home with nothing. Many found their farms and ranches in ruins. The only property they had left were the vast herds of cattle and horses scattered on the Texas prairies. With only a few small boys and old men to care for them during four years of war, the herds had spread all over the range. Many of the cattle had gone wild. Whoever could catch them could claim them.

Now so many millions of longhorns crowded the ranges that they were almost worthless. During and just after the war, there was hardly any place to sell Texas cattle. But in 1867, a market opened at Abilene, Kansas. Rumors about the prices paid there swept the southern cow country like wildfire. Steers worth three dollars or less in Texas, folks said, would sell for forty dollars apiece in Abilene. Why? Because it had a railroad. At Abilene, high-priced Texas steers could be loaded on freight cars bound for the beef-hungry cities of the North and East.

But Abilene was nearly eight hundred miles north of George's home in Goliad County, and the only way to get cattle there was to walk them across the raw, unknown plains of Indian

Territory (now Oklahoma). Cowboys needed a trail to guide them. They got it from a part-Cherokee trader named Jesse Chisholm. His wagon ruts marked a path through the territory that drovers could follow. They called it the Chisholm Trail.

Of course, the Kiowa, Comanche, and other tribes in the territory did not want Texas cowboys and thousands of longhorns invading their lands. To keep the northbound herds from trampling and eating the grass their own animals needed, they might attack.

Even though the cowmen around George's neighborhood knew the trail was risky, a few of the more daring decided to try it. In 1867 and 1868, they drove herds up to Abilene and east to Baxter Springs, Kansas, and other railroad towns where they hoped to find buyers. The warriors of the plains stopped some of them, stampeding herds and stealing the strays; or they demanded steers as payment for safe passage across their lands. But some drovers got through and sold their cattle. It was the first cash money they had made in many years, and getting it was worth the risk.

News of their success spread quickly. The excitement in the air made George tingle. He yearned to go on the long trek to Kansas. He ached to see the broad plains with their great buffalo herds. He pictured the maze of cattle pens at Abilene, and the fire-breathing, steam-belching railroad. He dreamed of meeting his first Kiowa warrior. But his parents wouldn't budge. They said he was too young for such hard and dangerous work.

George knew he might easily die on the trail. Cowboys, cattle, and horses could drown at river crossings, especially after heavy rains made the waters boil and churn. Quicksand formed deadly traps near rivers. Rain could turn the prairie to oozy mud that was almost as dangerous. Powerful thunderstorms spawned hail and lightning that could kill a cowboy caught in the open. Stampedes were always a threat. Any sudden noise—thunder, gunfire, the rattle of a pan at the chuckwagon—could send a herd rampaging in all directions. Even after searching for a whole day, the drovers might not find all of their cattle.

Cowboys on the trail had no tents. They had

no shelter except their blankets, nothing but their rolled-up rain slickers on which to rest their heads, no food except the beans, bacon, and biscuits the cook doled out from the chuck-wagon. They couldn't take anything with them except a change of clothes and a tin cup for coffee. Settlements and doctors were usually many miles away. Drovers who got hurt or sick might die before help could come.

But the dangers didn't stop the drives. Each year, more and more cowboys took to the trail. George and other boys rounded up thousands of cattle from the South Texas prairies. Cow-men who owned lots of beeves could make up a trail herd of two to three thousand animals, all wearing the same brand. Usually, though, several ranchers joined together to make a trail herd. The steers were given a "road brand" alongside their owner's brand to show which trail herd they belonged in. If they stampeded or got mixed up with another herd, the drovers could sort them by their road brands.

Some of the owners drove their herds north themselves. Others hired a trail boss and a crew of drovers to make the trip. They told the drovers where to take the cattle, then waved them off: "Adios, boys, I will see you in Abilene"—or in Ellsworth, Dodge City, or wherever the herd was heading. While the drovers pushed the cattle slowly up the trail, the owners hurried north to find buyers. Some waited at the markets for their herds to arrive. Others couldn't wait. They went back along the trail hundreds of miles to meet the drovers, taking buyers with them.

For two years after he quit school, George helped to gather and road-brand the northbound herds. He knew he could take care of

himself on the trail, but his parents still said no. They let his big brothers try it first. In 1870, Mat and Jack rode away with cattle going to Baxter Springs.

"Keep the rattlers out of your bed blankets!" George yelled as they left.

All the cowboys kidded about the poisonous snakes, Kiowa and Comanche raiders, deadly storms, and sleepless nights they faced on the northern drives. The danger and hardship didn't scare young Texas cowboys like George or his brothers. Trail driving was exciting— much more exciting than flushing stray cows

out of the Goliad County brush country. It seemed to George that that was all he did the whole time his brothers were gone.

When Mat and Jack returned home four months later, they told thrilling tales of Indians, stampedes, and buffalo hunts. Their stories fired George's wild desire to go up the trail, too. He didn't know it then, but he had caught an incurable case of "trail fever."

Up the "Chizzum" Trail

"No, sir, I won't sleep on watch," said George. He shook his head hard.

Trail boss Jim Byler looked him over. George knew what Mr. Byler was thinking: At seventeen, George was as tall as the boss. But was he tough enough to drive a herd to Kansas? Could he get up before daybreak and ride a horse all day? Could he stay awake for the midnight watch?

George wanted to go to Kansas more than anything. He had helped gather so many herds for the northern trail, his parents had finally said he could go on a drive. But Mr. Byler might not take him. Worried, George blurted, "Leastways, Mr. Byler, I won't sleep during stampedes or Indian fights."

A thin smile crossed the trail man's hard, windburned face. George looked him in the eye and waited for the answer. Finally the boss gave a short, quick nod.

"Whoopee!" George let out a shout that spooked the horses in the corral. He was going over the trail to Kansas! He thought this day in the spring of 1871 must be the happiest of his life. Everything had depended on Boss Byler's answer. After George's parents okayed the trip, a cowman named Monroe Choate had hired George as a drover. But they all gave Mr. Byler the final say. A trail boss wouldn't have a cowboy he didn't think could do the job.

George's outfit took charge of a thousand big, wild steers that belonged to the Choate & Bennett cattle company. Mr. Choate counted the steers and Boss Byler pointed them north. Then Mr. Choate waved them off.

"Adios, boys, I will see you in Abilene. . . ."

Before the thousand steers had gone many miles, trouble came. At the San Gabriel River, dark clouds gathered in the evening sky. A thunderstorm broke suddenly. The steers ran from the thunder and lightning as though they were being chased by wolves.

George raced through the storm with the stampeding herd. Lightning crackled all around. Soon he was lost. He didn't know this country at all. But he closed his mind to everything except staying with the cattle. He must not lose them! He was determined to prove to Boss Byler that he could do the job.

George rode all night and never dozed. He stuck with the runaways like a burr to horsehair. When dawn came, he was alone on the prairie with seventy-five steers. Calm now, the cattle grazed quietly.

Slowly George rode a circle around the steers. He studied their tracks. Hoofprints were everywhere. The trail left by the stampeding herd was too mixed up to read. George could not follow it back to the river, where the other cowboys probably were having breakfast about then.

He was tired and hungry. He had been awake all night and had not eaten since the day before. How long would it be before someone came to get him?

A lone horseman appeared on the horizon. *Mr. Byler missed me and sent a man to look for me!* George thought. Then, with a sinking feeling, he saw that the rider was Boss Byler himself.

"Are you awake?" Mr. Byler snapped as he rode up. "Why didn't you bring these cattle back to the herd?"

George explained that he couldn't follow the back trail. He figured he had best stay put, hold the strays where they were, and hope someone would come get him.

A muffled "Humph!" was Boss Byler's only reply. He helped George get the cattle headed in the right direction. It took them until four in the afternoon to reach the main herd.

George had kept his word not to sleep during stampedes. But after his wild ride through rain and mud, he needed a nap. He had been nearly two days in the saddle without rest. "Mr. Byler," George asked, "would it be all right if I slept until it's my turn to ride night herd?"

The trail boss surprised him. "Go eat and sleep all night; I will herd your relief," Mr. Byler said. "You deserve a rest."

George was tired down to his boots. But his spirits soared at the boss's words—until then, he had thought Mr. Byler was plenty mad.

After the stampede on the San Gabriel, the herd settled down and found its trail rhythm. The miles went by. Pausing often to graze, the cattle walked ten to twelve miles each day. At the Red River, they left Texas behind and struck the Chisholm Trail. They followed it north through Indian Territory.

George was thrilled when his outfit met up with Indians. Small bands of young Kiowas stampeded the cattle and held them for ransom. To get their stock back, the cowboys had to hand over several steers, supplies, and a few trinkets.

Just south of the Kansas line, George saw his first buffalo. About two hundred of the big, husky beasts grazed near the trail. Excited, all the drovers quit the herd and chased the buffaloes. George foolishly tried to rope a yearling. The young buffalo fought and lunged at the end of the rope with such strength that George had to turn it loose. Sadly he watched the yearling run away with his good rope looped around its neck.

The drovers got to Kansas late in May. They stopped by a creek about twenty miles from Abilene. The plains sprouted good spring grass. Steer buyers came out from Abilene to choose the animals they wanted and make their best deals. Once the price was agreed upon, some of the cowboys drove bunches of the cattle to the shipping pens in town. There the steers were loaded onto railroad cars that took them to the stockyards of Chicago.

One day George was on the prairie outside Abilene. He was herding cattle with another cowboy from South Texas named Ben Bor-

roum. George and Ben didn't notice when the cattle they were supposed to be watching strayed into a small patch of corn. The corn grew near a farm family's dugout. The steers trampled the new corn sprouts and crushed twenty baby chickens to death. The longhorns scared the farm folks so badly, the family ran and hid in the dugout.

It cost the Choate & Bennett cattle company, the boys' employer, about a hundred dollars to pay for the damage. After that, George and Ben watched their steers better.

When George's outfit had been in Kansas about a week, several more herds belonging to Choate & Bennett arrived. Most of the drovers who brought the herds up weren't needed anymore. It took fewer cowboys to herd cattle in

one place than to drive them over miles of prairie.

So George, Ben, and about fifty others made up an outfit and started back to Texas. They took a hundred and fifty extra horses, five chuckwagons, and five cooks with them.

The outfit headed south on the same trail their herds had followed north. When they reached the Washita River in Indian Territory, it was a raging torrent, deep and running fast. The spring rains had flooded the river. It was nearly three hundred yards to the other bank.

One of the older men took charge. He had seen flooded rivers before. He told the drovers to make a raft to ferry the wagons across. They didn't need anything fancy, just some logs roped together.

As the raft makers went to work, the man turned to the other cowboys. "Who's the best swimmer here?" he asked. "Somebody has to take a rope across to the other side so we can pull the raft over."

"I'll do it!" cried four cowboys at once. Each tried to swim a rope across the swollen river. Three got only halfway before turning back.

The fourth man made it to the far bank, but he lost hold of the rope in the heavy current.

George was the fifth to try. He took the end of the rope in his mouth, passed the rope over one shoulder, and jumped into the river. The other cowboys stood at the water's edge. They played out the line as he swam.

George fought the swift river every foot of the way. Finally he grabbed a willow limb and pulled himself onto the far bank. The rope was still between his teeth. He stood and waved his end of the line to let the others know he had made it.

"Yip-yip-yip-eeeee!" the cowboys shouted from the other side.

George felt ten feet tall. He was only seventeen years old, but he had made it when four others had failed. He had won the respect of the other drovers.

The cowboys worked quickly to tow the wagons across on the raft. Then they swam the horses over. Back on the trail, they hurried home to Texas. They crossed the Red River near the village of Denison and stayed in town long enough to visit all the stores and the saloons. Then they rode south to Denton. Because it was against the law to carry pistols inside the city limits of Denton, the local lawman ordered the cowboys to hand over their guns. Instead, the drovers whipped out their pistols, shot into the air, and raced out of town. The peace officer let them go—he was used to the wild ways of the Texas cowboy.

George's outfit also stopped at Fort Worth and every other town on the way back, but finally he reached Goliad County. The first thing George did when he got home was show off the pair of shop-made boots and two good suits of clothes he had bought in Kansas. One suit was black velvet. It had cost him fifty dollars, but he figured it was worth the money. All the girls liked the way it looked on him.

George was mighty satisfied with his first trip to Kansas. In five months on the trail, he'd had all the adventure he wanted—terrible thunderstorms, raging rivers, Indian raids, and midnight stampedes. He figured to be going up the trail again real soon.

Bandits!

Home from his Kansas adventure, George rested for a few days, then returned to his regular work on the range. Each spring, he helped to round up trail herds and start them north. Sometimes he rode with a herd only part of the way. Sometimes he went through to Kansas. Other times, he drove cattle south to the Texas Gulf Coast. There were packing plants on the coast that butchered thousands of cattle. The packeries wanted mainly the hides, which were made into ropes and whips, and the tallow, or fat, for candles and soap. They wasted most of the meat because there were no refrigerators or even ice to keep it fresh.

By the summer of 1874, George had made half a dozen cattle drives to Kansas or to the coast. He had crossed a dozen big rivers, including the mighty Red, which marked the top of Texas. He had seen floods on the Red keep ten thousand longhorns at bay, waiting for the waters to die down. A citizen of prairie and plain for all of his twenty years, he had finally seen his first real mountains, the Wichitas in Indian Territory.

Back in Goliad County he had his own home, and he was married. His wife was Rachel Reeves. Rachel had grown up on a ranch about twenty-five miles from the old Saunders place on Lost Creek. She and George married later than many folks: she was twenty-one and he was twenty. They started their own ranch south of his parents', near a stream called Goat Creek.

When he was home, George often rode with Captain Henry Scott's minutemen. They helped the local sheriff keep law and order. The volunteers were called "minute" men because they were ready to saddle up at a minute's notice to chase down outlaws and bandits. They protected the scattered ranches of South Texas from raiders who rode up out of Mexico.

Late one evening in June, at about ten o'clock, a horseman reined up short in front of George and Rachel's house. *"Bandidos!"* he cried. George hurried outside to meet him.

"They've caught the men who killed Thad Swift and his family!" the messenger said. Captain Fennessy, the leader of another company of minutemen, thought he had the cutthroats penned at the Moya ranch. The sheriff was headed there with a posse.

Everyone in the county knew about the Swift family's murder. Mexican raiders had killed them three nights earlier. People were scared. They pointed fingers at nearly every Mexican who lived nearby. Most of their Mexican neighbors were peaceful farmers and cattle raisers, no different from anyone else. But after the killings, George knew there would be trouble.

He kissed Rachel good-bye and went to saddle his horse. He rode to the Moya ranch with the sheriff and nine other men. The posse arrived at about eleven o'clock at night. They had covered the twelve miles from Goliad in one hour, and their horses were worn out.

Captain Fennessy's minutemen already had the Moya house surrounded. As the sheriff's posse rode up, one of Fennessy's men saw Señor Moya hiding in a field. The rider drew down on him with a gun. He was about to shoot when George stopped him.

"Wait!" George yelled. "You can't shoot that old man! He doesn't even have a gun. And we don't know if he had anything to do with the Swift murders."

Señor Moya was grateful to George for saving his life. He surrendered. The rest of the family stayed hidden inside their house. Its thick mud walls protected them from gunfire.

The standoff lasted for hours. Finally the sheriff promised the Moyas the protection of the law if they would give up. The Moyas thought they would be safe. They surrendered and came out of the house.

The sheriff and his posse started back to

Goliad with their prisoners. George rode with them. But they had gone only about three miles when Fennessy's men surrounded the posse. They shot and killed three of the prisoners, including old Señor Moya. In the wild shooting, a stray bullet hit George's horse.

George wasn't hurt in the attack. But the Moyas' murder made him furious. No one even knew whether they'd had anything to do with killing the Swift family. George made up his mind never to let such a thing happen again while he was around.

One night soon after the Moyas were shot, seventy-five or eighty men held a meeting. They wanted more revenge for the murder of the Swift family. They told each other they should kill every Mexican in "old Labardee," as they called the town of Goliad.

George had to stop the massacre. He stepped forward and began to speak. He was only twenty years old, but he made the other men stop their wild talking and listen to him.

"Men," he said, "most of you are older than I am and some of you may think that I am impertinent" (by that he meant bold or bad-

mannered) "in taking a stand against you. But you are about to do something that will bring you shame and that will put a blot on the history of Texas that can never be erased.

"If you go down there to old Labardee and massacre all the Mexicans, you will murder good men and innocent women," he went on. "You know that. You know that there are Mexican men and Mexican women who are as true and loyal and faithful as anybody ever was. You know that among the bad Mexicans at Labardee there are many good ones. In fact, there are more good ones than bad ones.

"I am in favor of dealing with the bad ones as they deserve," George said. "I will never take part in a wholesale butchery."

The men were quiet as George finished talking. He looked at them, then scratched a line in the dirt in front of him.

"Now," he dared them, "all of you that are in favor of using judgment and justice and that are against a massacre, step on this side of the line."

Every man stepped across. Many lives were saved that night because George had the courage to stand up for what he believed in.

Soon after, Captain Scott and his minute-men rode in from Mexico. They had a prisoner named Juan Flores. Flores was tried and found guilty of murdering the Swift family. The judge sentenced him to be hanged. George went home to Rachel, glad that the bloody business of revenge was over.

He put the trouble out of his mind. There was much violence and bloodshed in Texas after the Civil War, but George and Rachel didn't let it touch their home. They were happy together. Their ranch near Goat Creek was a peaceful hideaway. It had plenty of good grass and water for their herds. George was doing well in the cattle business. He loved the adventures of trail driving. But even more he loved being home with his family. He was thrilled when Rachel had their first baby, a year after they married. They named the child Johanna—Jonie for short. Two years later, another daughter, Georgia, was born. They also had a son named Dillard, but the baby died.

In 1880, when Jonie was five and Georgia was three, their mother got very sick. Worried, George bundled the family into the wagon. He took the girls to his parents. Then he drove

Rachel to San Antonio, ninety miles away over very rough roads, to see a doctor.

"Your wife will have to stay in the city for treatment," the doctor told him. "Her health is failing. She must have rest and proper medical care."

George knew he could never leave Rachel alone in the city. He had to be near her. There was only one thing to do: They would move to San Antonio and he would find a way to make a living there.

San Antonio in 1880 was a busy city of twenty thousand people. Seeing them rushing to and fro, George decided that they needed a cab service. He hurried back to Goliad County, sold his ranch, and returned to San Antonio with Jonie and Georgia. He used the money from his ranch to buy carriages and teams of horses. He kept them running day and night, carrying passengers all over the city.

But living in San Antonio did not help Rachel. The doctors could not cure her. After three years of treatment, she died of pneumonia one cold February morning in 1883.

Alone with two young daughters to raise, George thought he might settle for good in the city. With a partner named Harry Fawcett, he bought a livestock commission business. They took charge of horses and cattle that belonged to other people. They sold the livestock for the best price they could get. In return for selling the animals, the owners paid them part of the money from the sale.

Soon George and Harry were selling horses by the thousands. They bought a big herd for themselves. They planned to keep the horses until spring, then sell them to trail drivers going north to Kansas.

But when spring came, George and Harry found they couldn't sell their horses for as much as they thought the ponies were worth. George decided they would take the horses up the trail themselves. He had made only one drive in the four years he'd lived in San Antonio. He figured it was time to be moving again.

George left Jonie and Georgia with his parents. He and Harry sold their business in San Antonio. In April 1884, the partners gathered their horses, loaded their chuckwagon, and hit the trail for Dodge City, Kansas.

The Last Trail

A Kiowa warrior held George in an iron grip. Forty or fifty buffalo guns pointed at his head. George thought he was a goner.

The Indians were fighting mad. There were about two hundred of them facing only thirty-five trail drivers. If George didn't stay calm and talk fast, he would surely die. And many of his men would die with him.

The Kiowa band was led by Chief Bacon Rind. At first, the Kiowa said they would lead the drovers safely through their hunting

grounds if the cowboys would give them supplies from their chuckwagons.

Four Texas horse outfits were traveling together. They had caught up with each other
along the trail to Kansas. The drovers had bar-
gained with the Comanches for safe passage
just the day before. But Chief Bacon Rind's
Kiowa were harder to satisfy.

George had each outfit set down from its chuckwagon a sack of flour, ten pounds of coffee, ten tins of canned goods, five pounds of prunes, ten pounds of sugar, some bacon and beans, and a little of everything else they had. He also offered them two horses. The Kiowa did not accept. They wanted more food and more horses.

That made George mad. He told the cooks to put all the supplies back into the wagons. To the drovers he said, "Straddle your horses and start your herds."

George mounted his horse and began to ride off. Sitting tall in the saddle, he looked fierce. Strong, straight backed, blue eyed, with a neat mustache, he stood a little over six feet tall. He seemed even bigger on horseback.

But he didn't frighten the Kiowa. About a dozen warriors rushed him. Before he knew what was happening, they had him. They held his horse by the bridle. Buffalo guns pointed at him from all sides.

"It is not a pleasing sensation to have forty or fifty guns pointed at you with the fingers of mad Indians on the trigger," George would say later. "The boys from the four outfits rushed to my rescue with their pistols drawn, but I did not draw mine, as I knew it meant being made into mincemeat or cut up into doll rags."

George signaled to the cowboys to hold their fire. Then he started talking to the Kiowa in Spanish, English, and every Indian language he knew.

"You are making a big mistake," he told them. "You are going too far with this foolishness, and if you keep on I will send to Fort Sill for the bluecoats."

He was bluffing. There was no time to call out the soldiers from the fort. But the threat worked. The Kiowa lowered their guns and went away. The cowboys heaved sighs of relief and continued up the trail.

The four outfits drove on to Dodge City. George sold his horses, then returned to South Texas to see his girls. The visit was short because George had to leave for his second trail drive of the year.

In July 1884, he took a herd of cattle from far West Texas up the Pecos River to New Mexico Territory. Under the blazing summer sun, grass withered. There was no water for the cattle to drink. They were painfully thirsty, hot, dusty, and so weary that they barely could place one hoof in front of another. The waters of the Pecos had such a bad, salty taste, neither men nor cattle would drink from it, even as fiercely thirsty as they were. But the river valley made a good cattle trail, so

George followed it into New Mexico Territory. He delivered the herd to a place called Seven Rivers.

"It was a long, dry drive, and I was glad when through with it," was all George said when the trip was done.

In October, George began the last trail drive of his life. It would be the hardest of all.

He was to take a thousand heifers from West Texas to Arizona, more than four hundred miles away. The weather was turning cold. They would be heading through a rough, dry country of sagebrush flats, desert basins, steep-walled valleys, and jagged mountains. Geronimo was up in those mountains. The desert warrior and his band of a hundred and thirty Apache raiders refused to stay on the reservation. For ten years Geronimo had led his rebels on bloody raids against Mexican and American settlers, killing brutally, slashing throats, burning homesteads to the ground.

When George's outfit was ready, he called the men together. He warned them of the dangers they might face. But these were trail-tough Texas cowboys. Like George, they had ridden in freezing cold and blistering heat. In rain-storms and blizzards. In stampedes and floods. They had faced raiders and fought warring Indians. They knew what it was like to drive a herd through a desert that held no water, no grass, no shade. They were all good men on good horses. The herd was in good condition, too, the best of the lot—George had picked them himself.

In the morning, they pulled out.

George started them north to 8,750-foot Guadalupe Peak, then over the border into New Mexico Territory. They rested for a few days at Crow Springs. The drovers let the cattle drink their fill before moving on. None would drink again for more than a hundred miles of dry, broken desert.

The thousand heifers strung out in a ragged line. They walked for days without water. George drove them hard, night and day. He let them lie down and rest only when they could not keep moving. He had to get them to water as quickly as possible, or the whole herd would die in the desert.

The cattle were desperately thirsty when

they finally reached the mouth of the Sacramento River. But the river was a dry bed of gravel. The nearest water was another thirty miles up the canyon. Picking a path between towering bluffs, the heifers and their drovers straggled onward.

George was with the lead cattle when they first smelled water. They threw their heads up and sniffed the air like dogs scenting game. But they were too worn out even to trot. "They were in very poor condition and a pitiful sight to see, with their sunken eyes, and some of them barely able to creep along," George wrote later.

As fast as one bunch of heifers drank their fill from the river, the men turned the cattle up the steep bluff to make room for newcomers. It took about six hours to water the whole herd.

After a rest, the men drove the herd farther up the canyon, deep into the high-country wilderness. George saw his first wild elk and the tallest pine trees he had ever seen.

This was the land of Geronimo. At night, George and his men often saw Indian signal fires. If the Apaches wanted beef from the Texans' herd, they would probably attack while the cowboys slept. For the sake of his men, George decided to stay out of Geronimo's way. He had the cowboys bed the herd each evening and eat supper before it got dark. Then they took the horses and the chuckwagon and made camp a mile away from the cattle. That way, the Apaches would not find the drovers if they raided the herd.

It was nearly Christmas. The days were frosty, the nights bitter. But for a week the cowboys couldn't build a fire at night because the Apaches might see the flames. They slept in the freezing cold with only a few blankets to warm them. Each morning, their teeth chattering, they rounded up the herd and moved on.

Geronimo did not attack. George figured he left them alone because he didn't want to fight a bunch of hard-eyed Texas cowboys. Of course, he thought, the Apaches might not have wanted the Texans' thin, bony, half-starved cattle and horses.

The drovers pushed on, only a few miles each day. About halfway across New Mexico, fifty heifers got trapped in a bog and could not get out. George and his men roped each animal and urged their cow ponies back on their haunches, tightening the ropes, struggling to pull the heifers free. No matter how hard the horses and their riders pulled, they were unable to drag five of the cattle from the bog's deadly grip.

Beyond the small town of Tularosa, the herd slowly picked its way across lava beds and alkali flats. The weary cattle skirted the ranks of mountains that rose from the barren desert floor. They grazed the patches of scrubby desert grass that grew on the lower mountain slopes. There was nothing else for the herd to eat but cactus, sagebrush, and creosote bush. The cowboys sang as they pushed the cattle along. The men were numb with cold and exhaustion. Singing made them feel a little better and helped quicken the step of the worn-out beasts.

Finally they crossed the Rio Grande and stopped in the town of Magdalena. They were about three hundred miles from where they started. Two months outdoors in freezing weather had made George gravely ill. He couldn't go on. The owner of the herd met the drovers at Magdalena and took the cattle on to his ranch in Arizona himself.

When George was strong enough to travel, he went to El Paso, Texas, and got a job working cattle. A year later, in the spring of 1886, he went home to San Antonio.

And there he stayed. Now thirty-two years old, George quit the trail for good. He got Jonie and Georgia from their grandparents and moved them to San Antonio. He went back into the livestock commission business. He never again pointed a herd north to Kansas or west across the desert.

But for George it was not the end of the trail. He still had an important roundup to make. Only this one would be a roundup of men instead of cattle.

The Trail Drivers of Texas

The cattle trails were closed by 1895—only twenty-eight years after the first small herds had been driven north to the Kansas railheads. By then the open range was mostly fenced with barbed wire. The northern trails were cut off.

An exciting and colorful chapter in America's history was over. The world had never seen so many horsemen and cattle on the move over such a wide area. Nothing like it had ever happened before, and nothing like it would happen again.

George Saunders watched the trail-driving days come to an end. He began to worry that the trail drivers' story would be lost. The cowboys were growing old. When one of them died, everything he knew about trail talk and cowboy customs passed away with him.

"It would be the father of all mistakes to let their daring and valuable efforts be forgotten," George declared. So he went to work "rounding up" tales of the trail. He asked the old-time trail drivers to relate their memories so other people could read about their adventures.

George spent about five years gathering those stories. He hired an editor named J. Marvin Hunter to put them together. The result was a book of more than one thousand pages called *The Trail Drivers of Texas*. It was published during the 1920s. The book is as full of thrills and high excitement as the lives of the cowboys themselves.

No one but a lifelong cowman like George Saunders could have collected the stories of so many hundreds of old cowboys, horse wranglers, cattlemen, camp cooks, lawmen, Indian fighters, and other "cow people." It is probably the most important thing George did in his life. When he died on July 3, 1933, at age seventy-nine, he was remembered from San Antonio to New York City for bringing out the *Trail Drivers* book.

Today, we all know something about the trail-driving days and the old-time cowboy. In fact, when you think about the Old West, it's probably the hard-riding, slow-talking cowboy you think of first. Cowboy boots and a ten-gallon hat are symbols of America that people know around the world.

How did the cowboy get to be so famous in only twenty-eight years? People liked the romance of the cowboy's life. To many, he became the great American hero. Readers grabbed up books and articles about the trail-driving days. And later, cowboys starred in hundreds of action-packed movies and television shows.

Those stories didn't always stick to the facts. Much of what has been written and said about cowboys in the last one hundred years has

made them seem far better—or far worse—than they really were. Some stories make them knights on horseback, ready to die to stop a gang of rustlers. Others show them as trigger-happy outlaws who liked nothing better than to shoot up quiet little towns.

In *The Trail Drivers of Texas,* George Saunders gave the cowboys a chance to tell their own stories in their own words. Their stories reach across the years to tell us what life was really like for cowboys in the Old West. Reading those stories, we can go back in time.

Close your eyes and imagine those years long ago. Can you smell the campfire smoke, the boiling coffee, the scent of sagebrush? Listen—there's the squeak of saddle leather, the thud of a thousand hooves, the whinny of a cow pony. These things we will always have, because cowboys like George Saunders went up the northern trail and came home to tell the tale.

Selected Bibliography

George Saunders wrote much about his life as a trail driver. Many of his stories and articles appeared in the 1910s and 1920s in such magazines as *The Cattleman, The Pioneer Magazine of Texas,* and *Frontier Times.* His accounts are the basis for this biography. Events are presented as George described them.

Research for this book was done in the Texas State Archives, the Barker Texas History Center, and the Harry Ransom Humanities Research Center, Austin; the Old Trail Drivers Association of Texas Museum and the Daughters of the Republic of Texas Library, San Antonio; the Nita Stewart Haley Memorial Library and J. Evetts Haley History Center, Midland; and the Texas and Southwestern Cattle Raisers' Association Library, the William E. Jary, Jr., Historical Library, and the family papers of Roland Saunders Jary, Fort Worth.

The drawings were made on Arches cover paper with Conte sanguine sticks. The jacket was painted in oil on Arches paper.

BOOKS

Adams, Andy. *The Log of a Cowboy*. Boston: Houghton Mifflin, 1931.

Bushick, Frank H. *Glamorous Days*. San Antonio: Naylor, 1934.

Dobie, J. Frank. *A Vaquero of the Brush Country*. Austin: University of Texas Press, 1981.

Hunter, J. Marvin, ed. *The Trail Drivers of Texas.* Austin: University of Texas Press, 1985 (taken from the second edition revised, published in 1925 by George W. Saunders and Cokesbury Press).

Hunter, J. Marvin, Sr. *Peregrinations of a Pioneer Printer.* Grand Prairie, Tex.: Frontier Times Publishing House, 1954.

Wellman, Paul I. *The Trampling Herd.* Garden City, N. Y.: Doubleday, 1951.

Worcester, Don. *The Chisholm Trail.* Lincoln: University of Nebraska Press, 1980.

A quarter of a century of my life, from 1861 to 1886, was a continual chain of thrills, not by choice, but by the customs of those times. The dangers through which I passed during those days make me shudder when I recall them.

—*George W. Saunders*
Texas trail driver
1920